THE MASTERS

THE MASTERS

BY
ANNIE BESANT

GYAN

ISBN: 978-81-212-1918-1 (HB)
First Published, 1899
Published, 2018
Published by

Gyan Publishing House
5, Ansari Road
Daryaganj, New Delhi-110002
Phone: 011-47034999, 9811692060
www.gyanbooks.com
E-mail: books@gyanbooks.com

Printed at: G. Print Process, Delhi.

FOREWORD

EVER the idea of the Masters of the White Lodge, the Elder Brothers of Humanity, sends a thrill through the human heart, and any words about Them are eagerly and gladly welcomed. The idea of there being anything grotesque in the conception of these great Beings, these perfected Men, has quite passed away from the West, as though it had not been. It is now realised that the existence of such Beings is natural, and that, given evolution, these highest products of evolution are a natural necessity. Many are beginning to see in the grandiose figures of the past, evidence that such Men are, and as reason recognises Them in the past, hope springs forward to find Them in the present.

More: there is an increasing number of persons amongst us, both in the East and the West, who have succeeded in finding the Masters, and from whose minds, therefore, doubt of Their existence has for ever been swept away. The Way to Them is open, and those who seek shall find.

May this booklet arouse some to the seeking of the great Teachers. I, who know Them, can do no greater service to my brethren, than to inspire them to begin a search which will give them a prize beyond all telling.

ANNIE BESANT

CONTENTS

THE PERFECT MAN

PERFECT MAN: A LINK IN THE CHAIN OF EVOLUTION

THERE is a stage in human evolution which immediately precedes the goal of human effort, and when this stage is passed through, man, as man, has nothing more to accomplish. He has become perfect; his human career is over. The great religions bestow on this Perfect Man different names, but, whatever the name, the same idea is beneath it; He is Mithra, Osiris, Kṛṣhṇa, Buḍḍha, Christ—but He ever symbolises the Man made perfect. He does not belong to a single religion, a single nation, a single human family; He is not stifled in the wrappings of a single creed; everywhere He is the most noble, the most perfect ideal. Every religion proclaims Him; all creeds have in Him their justification; He is the ideal towards which every belief strives, and each religion fulfils effectively its mission according to the clearness with which it illumines, and the precision with which it teaches the road whereby He may be reached. The name of Christ, used for the Perfect

Man throughout Christendom, is the name of a *state*, more than the name of a *man*; "Christ in you, the hope of glory," is the Christian teacher's thought. Men, in the long course of evolution, reach the Christ state, for all accomplish in time the centuried pilgrimage, and He with whom the name is specially connected in Western lands is one of the "Sons of God" who have reached the final goal of humanity. The word has ever carried the connotation of a state; it is "the anointed". Each must reach the state: "Look within thee; thou art Buḍḍha." "Till the Christ be formed in you."

As he who would become a musical artist should listen to the masterpieces of music, as he should steep himself in the melodies of the master-artists, so should we, the children born of humanity, lift up our eyes and our hearts, in ever-renewed contemplation, to the mountains, on which dwell the Perfect Men of our race. What we are, They were; what They are, we shall be. All the sons of men can do what a Son of Man has accomplished, and we see in Them the pledge of our own triumph; the development of like divinity in us is but a question of evolution.

COMMANDS: OUTER AND INNER

I have sometimes divided interior evolution into sub-moral, moral, and super-moral; sub-moral, wherein the distinctions between right and wrong are not seen, and man follows his desires, without question, without scruple; moral, wherein right and wrong are seen, become ever more defined and inclusive, and obedience to law is striven after; super-moral, wherein external law is transcended, because the divine nature rules its vehicles. In the moral condition, law is recognised as a legitimate barrier, a salutary restraint; "Do this"; "Avoid that"; the man struggles to obey, and there is a constant combat between the higher and lower natures. In the super-moral state the divine life in man finds its natural expression without external direction; he loves, not because he ought to love, but because he is love. He acts, to quote the noble words of a Christian Initiate, "not after the law of a carnal commandment, but by the power of an endless life". Morality is transcended when all the powers of the man turn to the Good as the magnetised needle turns to the north; when divinity in man seeks ever the best for all. There is no more combat, for the victory is won; the Christ has reached His perfect stature only when He has become the Christ triumphant, Master of life and death.

THE FIRST INITIATION

This stage of the Christ-life, the Buddha-life, is entered by the first of the great Initiations, in which the Initiate is "the little child," sometimes the "babe," sometimes the "little child, three years old". The man must "regain the child-state he hath lost"; he must "become a little child" in order to "enter the kingdom". Passing through that portal, he is born into the Christ-life, and, treading the "way of the Cross," he passes onwards through the successive gateways on the Path; at the end, he is definitely liberated from the life of limitations, of bondage, he dies to time to live in eternity, and he becomes conscious of himself as life rather than as form.

There is no doubt that in early Christianity this stage of evolution was definitely recognised as before every individual Christian. The anxiety expressed by S. Paul that Christ might be born in his converts bears sufficient testimony to this fact, leaving aside other passages that might be quoted; even if this verse stood alone it would suffice to show that in the Christian ideal the Christ-stage was regarded as an inner condition, the final period of evolution for every believer. And it is well that Christians should recognise this, and not regard the life of the disciple, ending in the Perfect Man, as an exotic, planted in Western soil, but native only in far Eastern lands. This ideal is part of all true and spiritual Christianity, and the birth of the Christ in each Christian soul is the object of Christian teaching. The very object of religion is to bring about this birth, and if it could be that this mystic teaching could slip out of Christianity, that faith could no longer raise to divinity those who practise it.

The first of the great Initiations is the birth of the Christ, of the Buḍḍha, in the human consciousness, the transcending of the I-consciousness, the falling away of limitations. As is well known to all students, there are four degrees of development covered by the Christ-stage, between the thoroughly good man and the triumphant Master. Each of these degrees is entered by an Initiation, and during these degrees of evolution consciousness is to expand, to grow, to reach the limits possible within the restrictions imposed by the human body. In the first of these, the change experienced is the awakening of consciousness in the spiritual world, in the world where consciousness identifies itself with the life, and ceases to identify itself with the forms in which the life may at the moment be imprisoned. The characteristic of this awakening is a feeling of sudden expansion, and of widening out beyond the habitual limits of the life, the recognition of a Self, divine and puissant which is life, not form; joy, not sorrow; the feeling of a marvellous peace, passing all of which the world can dream. With the falling away of limitations comes an increased intensity of life, as though life flowed in from every side rejoicing over the barriers removed, so vivid a feeling of reality that all life in a form seems as death, and earthly light as darkness. It is an expansion so marvellous in its nature, that consciousness feels as though it had never known itself before, for all it had regarded as consciousness is as unconsciousness in the presence of this upwelling life. Self-consciousness, which commenced to germinate in child-humanity, which has developed, grown, expanded ever within the limitations of form, thinking itself separate, feeling ever "I," speaking ever of "me" and "mine"—this Self-consciousness suddenly feels all selves as Self, all forms as common property. He sees that limitations were necessary for the building of a centre of Selfhood in which Self-identity might persist, and at the same time he feels that the form is only an instrument he uses while he himself, the living consciousness, is one in all that lives. He knows the full meaning of the oft-spoken phrase the "unity of humanity," and feels what it is to live in all that lives and moves, and this consciousness is accompanied with an immense joy, that joy of life which even in its faint reflections upon earth is one of the keenest ecstasies known to man. The unity is not only seen by the intellect, but it is felt as satisfying the yearning for union which all know who have loved; it is a unity felt from within, not seen from without; it is not a conception but a life.

In many pages of old, but ever on the same lines, has the birth of the Christ in man been figured. And yet how all words shaped for the world of forms fail to image forth the world of life.

But the child must grow into the perfect man, and there is much to do, much weariness to face, many sufferings to endure, many combats to wage, many obstacles to overcome, ere the Christ born in the feebleness of infancy may reach the stature of the Perfect Man. There is the life of labour among his brother-men; there is the facing of ridicule and suspicion; there is the delivery of a despised message; there is the agony of desertion, and the passion of the cross, and the darkness of the tomb. All these lie before him in the path on which he has entered.

By continual practice, the disciple must learn to assimilate the consciousness of others, and to centre his own consciousness in life, not in form, so that he may pass beyond the "heresy of separateness," which makes him regard others as different from himself. He has to expand his consciousness by daily practice, until its normal state is that which he temporarily experienced at his first Initiation. To this end he will endeavour in his everyday life to identify his consciousness with the consciousness of those with whom he comes into contact day by day; he will strive to feel as they feel, to think as they think, to rejoice as they rejoice, to suffer as they suffer. Gradually he must develop a perfect sympathy, a sympathy which can vibrate in harmony with every string of the human lyre. Gradually he must learn to answer, as if it were his own, to every sensation of another, however high he may be or however low. Gradually, by constant practice, he must identify himself with others in all the varied circumstances of their different lives. He must learn the lesson of joy and the lesson of tears, and this is only possible when he has transcended the separated self, when he no longer asks aught for himself, but understands that he must henceforth live in life alone.

His first sharp struggle is to put aside all that up to this point has been for him life, consciousness, reality, and walk forth alone, naked, no longer identifying himself with any form. He has to learn the law of life, by which alone the inner divinity can manifest, the law which is the antithesis of his past. The law of form is taking; the law of life is giving. Life grows by pouring itself out through form, fed by the inexhaustible source of life at the heart of the universe; the more the life pours itself out the greater the inflow from within. It seems at first to the young Christ as though all his life were leaving him, as though his hands were left empty after outpouring their gifts on a thankless world; only when the lower nature has been definitely sacrificed is the eternal life experienced, and that which seemed the death of being is found to be a birth into a fuller life.

THE SECOND INITIATION

Thus consciousness develops, until the first stage of the path is trodden, and the disciple sees before him the second Portal of Initiation, symbolised in the Christian Scriptures as the Baptism of the Christ. At this, as he descends into the waters of the world's sorrows, the river that every Saviour of men must be baptised in, a new flood of divine life is poured out upon him; his consciousness realises itself as the Son, in whom the life of the Father finds fit expression. He feels the life of the Monad, his Father in Heaven, flowing into his consciousness, and realises that he is one, not with men only, but also with his heavenly Father, and that he lives on earth only to be the expression of the Father's will, His manifested organism. Henceforth is his ministry to men the most patent fact of his life. He is the Son, to whom men should listen, because from him the hidden life flows forth, and he has become a channel through which that hidden life can reach the outer world. He is the priest of the Mystery God, who has entered within the veil, and comes forth with the glory shining from his face, which is the reflection of the light in the sanctuary.

It is there that he begins that work of love symbolised in the outer ministry by his willingness to heal and to relieve; round him press the souls seeking light and life, attracted by his inner force and by the divine life manifested in the accredited Son of the Father. Hungry souls come to him, and he gives them bread; souls suffering from the disease of sin come, and he heals them by his living word; souls blinded by ignorance come, and he illuminates them by wisdom. It is one of the signs of a Christ in his ministry, that the abandoned and the poor, the desperate and the degraded, come to him without the sense of separation. They feel a welcoming sympathy and not a repelling; for kindness radiates from his person, and the love that understands flows out around him. Truly the ignorant know not that he is an evolving Christ, but they feel a power that raises, a life which vitalises, and in his atmosphere they inbreathe new strength, new hope.

THE THIRD INITIATION

The third Portal is before him, which admits him to another stage of his progress, and he has a brief moment of peace, of glory, of illumination, symbolised in Christian writings by the Transfiguration. It is a pause in his life, a brief cessation of his active service, a journey to the Mountain whereon broods the peace of heaven, and there—side by side with some who have recognised his evolving divinity—that divinity shines forth for a moment in its transcendent beauty. During this lull in the combat, he sees his future; a series of pictures unrolls before his eyes; he beholds the sufferings which lie before him, the solitude of Gethsemane, the agony of Calvary. Thenceforth his face is set steadfastly towards Jerusalem, towards the darkness he is to enter for the love of mankind. He understands that ere he can reach the perfect realisation of unity he must experience the quintessence of solitude. Hitherto, while conscious of the growing life, it has seemed to him to come to him from without; now he is to realise that its centre is within him; in solitude of heart he must experience the true unity of the Father and the Son, an interior and not an outer unity, and then the loss even of the Father's Face; and for this all external contact with men, and even with God, must be cut off, that within his own Spirit he may find the One.

THE DARK NIGHT OF THE SOUL

As the dark hour approaches, he is more and more appalled by the failure of the human sympathies on which he has been wont to rely during the past years of life and service, and when, in the critical moment of his need, he looks around for comfort and sees his friends wrapt in indifferent slumber, it seems to him that all human ties are broken, that all human love is a mockery, all human faith a betrayal; he is flung back upon himself to learn that only the tie with his Father in heaven remains, that all embodied aid is useless. It has been said that in this hour of solitude the soul is filled with bitterness, and that rarely a soul passes over this gulf of voidness without a cry of anguish; it is then that bursts forth the agonised reproach: "Couldst thou not watch with me one hour?"—but no human hand may clasp another in that Gethsemane of desolation.

When this darkness of human desertion is overpast, then, despite the shrinking of the human nature from the cup, comes the deeper darkness of the hour when a gulf seems to open between the Father and the Son, between the life embodied and the life infinite. The Father, who was yet realised in Gethsemane when all human friends were slumbering, is veiled in the passion of the Cross. It is the bitterest of all the ordeals of the Initiate, when even the consciousness of the life of sonship is lost, and the hour of the hoped-for triumph becomes that of the deepest ignominy. He sees his enemies exultant around him; he sees himself abandoned by his friends and his lovers; he feels the divine support crumble away beneath his feet; and he drinks to the last drop the cup of solitude, of isolation, no contact with man or God bridging the void in which hangs his helpless soul. Then from the heart that feels itself deserted even by the Father rings out the cry: "My God! my God! why hast *Thou* forsaken me?"

Why this last proof, this last ordeal, this most cruel of all illusions? Illusion, for the dying Christ is nearest of all to the divine Heart.

Because the Son must know himself to be one with the Father he seeks, must find God not only within him but as his innermost Self; only when he knows that the Eternal is himself and he the Eternal, is he beyond the possibility of the sense of separation. Then, and then only, can he perfectly help his race, and become a conscious part of the uplifting energy.

THE GLORY OF PERFECTION

The Christ triumphant, the Christ of the Resurrection and Ascension, has felt the bitterness of death, has known all human suffering, and has risen above it by the power of His own divinity. What now can trouble His peace, or check His outstretched hand of help? During his evolution He learned to receive into Himself the currents of human troubles and to send them forth again as currents of peace and joy. Within the circle of His then activity, this was His work, to transmute forces of discord into forces of harmony. Now He must do it for the world, for the humanity out of which He has flowered. The Christs and their disciples, each in the measure of his evolution, thus protect and help the world, and far bitterer would be the struggles, far more desperate the combats of humanity, were it not for the presence of these in its midst, whose hands bear up "the heavy karma of the world".

Even those who are at the earliest stage of the Path become lifting forces in evolution, as in truth are all who unselfishly work for others, though these more deliberately and continuously. But the Christ triumphant does completely what others do at varying stages of imperfection, and therefore is He called a "Saviour," and this characteristic in Him is perfect. He saves, not by substituting Himself for us, but by sharing with us His life. He is wise, and all men are the wiser for His wisdom, for His life flows into all men's veins and pulses, in all men's hearts. He is not tied to a form, nor separate from any. He is the Ideal Man, the Perfect Man; each human being is a cell in His body, and each cell is nourished by His life.

Surely it had not been worth while to suffer on the Cross and to tread the Path that leads thereto, simply to win a little earlier His own liberation, to be at rest a little sooner. The cost would have been too heavy for such a gain, the strife too bitter for such a prize. Nay, but in his triumph humanity is exalted, and the path trodden by all feet is rendered a little shorter. The evolution of the whole race is accelerated; the pilgrimage of each is made less long. This was the thought that inspired Him in the violence of the combat, that sustained his strength, that softened the pangs of loss. Not one being, however feeble, however degraded, however ignorant, however sinful, who is not a little nearer to the light when a Son of the Highest has finished His course. How the speed of evolution will be quickened as more and more of these Sons rise triumphant, and enter into conscious life eternal. How swiftly will turn the wheel which lifts man into divinity as more and more men become consciously divine.

THE INSPIRING IDEAL

Herein lies the stimulus for each of us who, in our noblest moments, have felt the attraction of the life poured out for love of men. Let us think of the sufferings of the world that knows not why it suffers; of the misery, the despair of men who know not why they live, and why they die; who, day after day, year after year, see sufferings fall upon themselves and others and understand not their reason; who fight with desperate courage, or who furiously revolt against conditions they cannot comprehend or justify. Let us think of the agony born of blindness, of the darkness in which they grope, without hope, without aspiration, without knowledge of the true life, and of the beauty beyond the veil. Let us think of the millions of our brothers in the darkness, and then of the uplifting energies born of our sufferings, our struggles, and our sacrifices. We can raise them a step towards the light, alleviate their pains, diminish their ignorance, abridge their journey towards the knowledge which is light and life. Who of us that knows even a little, that will not give himself for these who know naught?

We know by the Law immutable, by Truth unswerving, by the endless Life and God, that all divinity is within us, and that though it be now but little evolved, all is there of infinite capacity, available for the uplifting of the world. Surely then there is not one, able to feel the pulsing of the Divine Life, that is not attracted by the hope to help and bless. And if this Life be felt, however feebly, for however brief a time, it is because in the heart there is the first thrill of that which will unfold as the Christ-life, because the time approaches for the birth of the Christ-babe, because in such a one humanity is seeking to flower.

THE MASTERS AS FACTS AND IDEALS[1]

THE PLACE OF THE FIGHTER

MR. SINNETT AND FRIENDS—Almost a year ago I stood on this same platform to address, in this hall, an audience on my return from the Indian land. Since then much has happened. Myself I have travelled far and wide—to the other side of the world, to the lands that we may say lie beneath our feet; back from those lands to India, and travelling through India once again from the South to the farthest North; and then back again from India here, knowing that while I was away there had been much of attack, much of difficulty, much of disturbance; hearing first a rumour in the far-off Antipodes of doubt and of challenge, of so-called exposure, and of virulent abuse. And then when I came nearer, as far as India, gaining more particulars, hearing details of the attack, but still too far away to take effective part in the struggle, and, bound by other duty, unable to come at once back to the land

[1] A lecture delivered in 1895. Chairman: Mr. A. P. Sinnett.

where, outwardly at least, the struggle was at its hottest. When the time came that engagements permitted me to return, when the time came that once again I could stand in this hall to face an English audience, I thought it well to choose for my subject that point round which the reality of the attack had raged, and to take up in the first words that I should speak in this country, the most really important matter at which the comments had been levelled while I was away.

For I know that wherever there is difficulty there is the place where the brave soldier should be found; and I did not forget that a writer in our English tongue had spoken of some who stood by religion when she walked in silver slippers in the sunshine amid applause, but were ashamed to stand beside her in shadow and under outrage, ashamed when she was clothed in rags instead of in purple. But I have learned in a stormy life that the moment for defence is the moment of attack; that not when there is sunshine is one's word so necessary as when the storm-clouds gather and when difficulties are on every side. For the time to be loyal to truth is when truth is attacked; the time to be faithful to knowledge is when knowledge is assailed; and I should deem that those of us who know the truth of the existence of the Mahāṭmās were traitors to truth and renegades to their responsibility, if they allowed themselves to be silent because laughed into silence by ridicule, or allowed themselves to deny their knowledge because the fact with which that knowledge is connected has been outraged by fraud and assailed by unfair dealing. Therefore, I choose the subject for my first address; therefore I come to lay before you evidence that I think worthy of your consideration, and to ask for it your patient attention and your thoughtful and deliberate weighing.

THE TESTIMONY OF RELIGIONS

"The Masters, as Facts and Ideals."—I have taken the double title, for there are some who know Them not as facts, to whom yet the ideal is valuable, precious, and inspiring. Not every member of our Society believes in the existence of Mahāṭmās. There are many and many who are within the limits of the Society who have no knowledge and no belief upon the subject; and it is the rule of our Society that no declaration of faith shall be asked from anyone who enters, save in the Brotherhood of man, without the distinctions that on the surface are set up. So that within the limits of the Society you may have alike believer and non-believer in the present existence or the past existence of these great Teachers. But I, who believe in Them, and know Them to exist, speak here not in the name of the Society which has no creed, but in my own and in the name of others who share this belief or this knowledge with myself; and before you I am going to place what I believe to be rational evidence worthy of consideration—evidence that you can think over at leisure and make up your minds upon as you will; and I speak also for the sake of the ideal, for the ideals of the race are precious, and cannot lightly be either outraged or denied. For great is this ideal of the Mahāṭmā, despite the idle laughter that has been used—for the name is merely the Samskṛṭ for Great Spirit —despite the laughter and the ridicule and the foolish talk which have gathered round the name. This mockery is a danger to a great ideal, valuable far beyond the bounds of the Theosophical Society.

For there is not one great religion that has raised and elevated the minds of men, there is not one mighty faith that has led millions to a knowledge of the spiritual life and the possibilities of human growth, there is not one that has not founded that belief on a Divine Man, there is not one that does not look back, as its Founder, to one of these mighty Souls who have brought knowledge of spiritual truth to the world. Look back to the past as you will, take what faith you choose. Every one of them is founded on this same ideal, and looks backward for its Teacher to a Man who is divine in His life. Around this ideal gather all the hopes of men, around this ideal gather the future destinies of humanity. For unless man be a spiritual Being, unless he have within himself the possibility of spiritual unfoldment, unless there be some evidence available that men have become perfect, that it is not only a dream of the future, but a reality which the race has already realised, unless it be true that for you and for me there are open the same mighty possibilities that have been proved possible in the past by those who have achieved, then the hopes of men rest on no foundation, the longings of men after perfection have in them no certainty of realisation, humanity remains but the thing of a day, instead of being heir to a boundless immortality. That man may become divine, that it is which has inspired the greatest of our race, which has cheered the miserable in their agony, and has glorified the future with a hope which is not a lie. That is why I defend the ideal. For what is the Mahāṭmā? He is the man who has become perfect, He is the man who has reached union with the Divine, He is the man who by slow degrees has developed the possibilities of the spiritual nature, and stands triumphant where we are struggling to-day. Every religion, I said, has borne witness to Him. You find that every religion of the world looks back to a Divine Teacher. You may have the name of Zoroaster in Persia, of Manu in India, of the Buḍḍha in later days, of the Christ in Palestine, every one of them the Divine Man, who has brought the certainty of human perfection to those who have come within the range of His influence. That is the ideal which is being outraged to-day, and for the sake of that ideal it is that I stand to speak before you to-night.

A THEORY

And now what shall be the line of our evidence? I propose first to suggest that the theory is a probable theory on the lines of natural evolution; that very briefly, in order to lead the way to the positive evidence. Then I propose to turn to the evidence for the existence of these perfected Divine Men in the past; then to come on from that to the evidence for Their existence in the present; then—because without this last part the lecture would remain unpractical for us—then to show how it is possible for men to become perfect, a slight sketch at least of the methods by which the Divine Man becomes.

First, then, for the theory that the existence of Masters is in itself probable and in accordance with the analogy of nature as we see it around us, as we know it in the past. Few to-day, probably, will dispute the fact of evolution. Few will deny that our race progresses, and that cycle after cycle you will find nations advancing and reaching higher and higher pinnacles of knowledge, higher and higher pinnacles in growth and in development. Theoretically there is nothing impossible or absurd in the theory that taking into consideration the vast periods of time which have elapsed since man first trod this earth, taking into consideration the enormous differences that we see to-day between the lowest savage and the highest man as he is generally known, taking these differences in the present, and the vast spaces of time for evolution that lie behind us in the past, it is not, at least, irrational or absurd that there may have been evolution carried to a point in the case of some individuals as much above the evolution of the higher civilised man of to-day, as he is higher than the lowest type of savage in existence still.

Nor is that all. It is not only that we have enormous ranges of time behind us, but that there are traces of mighty civilisations which show that the race had climbed high in knowledge, high in philosophy, high in science and in religion, thousands upon thousands of years ago, nay! I might say centuries of thousands of years. For looking backwards you see traces of mighty civilisations which imply the presence of men of a most advanced type, and it is scarcely rational to suppose that the so much talked-of evolution has been nothing more than a mere ebb and flow, leaving nothing as result, nothing more than successive periods of high civilisation and then of utter barbarism, and civilisation again re-begun with no links to preserve continuity of knowledge. It is not at least impossible, and in a moment we shall see signs that it is probable, that out of that mighty past some will have grown upwards, advancing higher and higher and perfecting the human race in individuals, as slowly the general race will in its turn become perfect. Not impossible, not even improbable, remembering that progress is the law of nature, and the vast spaces of time during which humanity has lived.

HISTORICAL EVIDENCE

But from that mere possibility, which I take because it is well to clear out of the way at the outset the idea that the theory is in itself impossible and absurd, turning from that mere possibility, let us take historical evidence and let us see whether history does not, from time to time, show some gigantic human figures which stand out above and beyond the men of their time and the ordinary height of humanity; whether there is not evidence which cannot be denied that such Men are not merely the products of popular imagination, that They are not merely men of the past, exaggerated by popular tradition and seen magnified, as it were, through the haze of centuries. I speak of those Great Ones to whom I alluded who have been the Founders of the great religions of the world. It is not only that there is unbroken tradition, and that the religions remain which these Men builded, but there is more than tradition, there is more than a religion which has grown; there is a literature, marked, definite, distinct, whose antiquity no scholar denies, although some may claim for it a vaster antiquity than others may be ready to concede. Take the later dates; they will serve my purpose, though I do not regard them as accurate. Take the later dates that would be given you by the Orientalists who have studied the literature of China, of Persia, of India, to say nothing of later times. You have there certain books regarded as sacred, books for which the religion has claimed what may fairly be termed an immemorial antiquity. You have amongst the Chinese their ancient sacred books; you have amongst the Pārsīs, the followers of Zoroaster, their books, also now translated into your own tongue. You have from India the Veḍas, the Upanishaṭs, to say nothing of the later works, and I might, without possibility of challenge, give you long lists of mighty works which are held as Scriptures by the believers in these faiths. Who wrote those works, and whence the knowledge? That they exist is obvious. That they must have authors can scarcely be denied. And yet those works from a far-off antiquity show a depth of spiritual knowledge, a depth of philosophic thought, a depth of insight into human nature, and a depth of moral teaching so magnificent, that the greatest minds of our own day, both in morals and in philosophy, must admit that those writings are greater than they can produce, and that the modern world can show nothing which even approaches them in sublimity.

It is not a question of tradition, but of books; not a question of theory, but of fact; for if the books are so great, the morality so pure, the philosophy so sublime, and the knowledge so vast, their authors must have had the knowledge which therein you find incorporated. And the testimony of millions upon millions of human beings answers to the reality of the spiritual truth, and nations are guided by the teachings that thus have come down. Nor is that all. These teachings are similar wherever you find them. The same teaching of the unity of the Divine Life out of which the universe has grown; the same teaching of the identity of the Spirit in man with the Spirit from which the universe has come; the same teaching that man by certain methods may develop the spiritual Life in himself and come into positive knowledge of divinity, and not only hope and faith. So that you have, coming down from far-off times, at least this fact which cannot be denied: that some men lived in the far-off past whose thought was great enough, whose morality was pure enough, whose philosophy was sublime enough, to outlast the wrecks of civilisation and the destructive force of time, and that to-day your Orientalists are translating for the teaching of the modern world that which mighty men of old once taught, and find the grandest thoughts to which the race has given birth in these Scriptures that have come down from the most ancient times.

That some then have lived far greater than ourselves, that some have lived whose knowledge goes far beyond the knowledge that we possess, that we still learn in philosophy and in spiritual matters from these far-off Teachers who spoke millenniums ago; that is a fact that cannot be denied. That there have been Divine Men in the past that we speak of as Mahāṭmās, that they have left the testimony to Their existence in this mighty and sublime literature, that is the first line of argument—the establishment of the existence in the past, the proof that such Men have lived and have taught, and that by Their teaching They have guided and helped millions of the human race. That Their teaching has been identical in its main outlines, that Their teaching is identical in its moral force, that the spiritual truths enunciated have come down unchanged through the centuries: so far, at least, can we speak with certainty, the ground so far is solid beneath our feet.

The statements in this literature appeal to human experience. They not only say that certain things are, but they say these things can be known. They not only declare the reality of the Soul, but they say that that reality can be proved; so that the teaching stands in this position, that it announces certain alleged facts which remain verifiable for all time, thereby affording a continually accumulating proof of the reality of the knowledge of Those who first gave the statements to the world.

FIRST-HAND EXPERIENCE

Pass from that to the next point in the argument—that these statements have been verified by experience and are being verified to-day. Take, for instance, such a land as India. There you have an unbroken tradition, a tradition which comes down to the present time, a tradition that there always have been Teachers who may be found, Teachers who possess the knowledge which is hinted at in the books of which I speak, who can add the practical teaching to the theoretical statement, and enable people to verify by experiment that which is said to be true in the literature to which I have alluded. Ask any Indian of to-day what is his belief on this question, and he will tell you, if he has not been westernised, and you can gain his confidence, that always in his land there has remained the belief that these Men have existed in the past and have not passed out of existence in the present; that They have more and more withdrawn from the ordinary haunts of men, that They have become more and more difficult to discover as materiality has made its way and spirituality has diminished; but that still They can occasionally be found, that still the first steps of the Path are open.

And not only is there that belief, but you will find scattered throughout India many, many men who, while they have not reached the point of Mahāṭmāship, have taken certain steps above the physical plane, and have developed in themselves powers and capacities which the ordinary Westerner would look on as absolutely impossible of attainment. I do not now speak of the Mahāṭmās, but of the hundreds of so-called yogis scattered through the jungles and the mountains of India, some of whom habitually exercise remarkable powers—powers which here would seem incredible, but of which there is ever-accumulating testimony coming to you from the mouths of travellers who collect and who record the facts with which they themselves have come in contact. For the earlier stages of the development of the inner man are not so difficult of attainment, and in a country like India, where there is not the difficulty of scepticism to overcome, because there the belief has existed for thousands of years, you will find many and many a man who exercises the lower psychical powers, and a few who have gone far beyond that stage and exercise either the higher psychic faculties or the really spiritual powers of man.

And you can find some who have personal experience, some who have individual knowledge of Teachers, of Masters, who train Their pupils in the higher path of what is called the Rāja, or the Kingly, Yoga, that is, the Yoga which primarily trains the mind rather than the body, which works by concentration of the mind, by meditation and by the evolution of the higher mental faculties, on which there is so much discussion here, and who by a definite system of training are able to consciously use powers of the mind which enable the possessor to pass beyond physical limitations, and passing out of the body to receive instruction which he is able then to bring back to the lower consciousness and impress on the physical brain, proving by his knowledge the reality of his teaching, and proving the existence of his Master by his knowledge which from Him he has obtained.

That then would be the next line of evidence available. Not available, you may fairly retort, to the majority of yourselves. But then you are surely bound to remember, as reasonable men and women, that if you desire knowledge you must seek it where the knowledge is to be found, and that it is as absurd for a number of men, who have never investigated, who have never even tried to investigate, who have never travelled, to sit here in a London office and write on that of which they have no knowledge, as it would be for some ignorant Indian, who has never had the slightest experience of your Western experiments, say in the Royal Institution, to sit down and declare that those are absolutely impossible and ludicrous, because he himself has not travelled here and has not had the opportunity of seeing them performed. You must deal with evidence on rational lines, and if you cannot yourselves come into contact with certain acts, with certain phases of human life, you must either remain ignorant—and then you should be silent—or you should take the testimony of those who have carefully investigated, and have laid the result of their investigations before you.

HOW CAN WE FIND THE MASTERS?

And that leads me to my next line of argument. Suppose such Men existed in the past, suppose we admit, as every religion admits for its own Founder—though it may deny as to the Founders of other religions—suppose we admit that in the past Divine Men have lived, suppose that, believing in the immortality of the Spirit, we are bound to admit that They must still exist somewhere if They ever existed at all; then the next question will be: Do these Men of the past exist in the present? Can They be reached?

Can They be known? And are there others who have reached a similar point, whose existence may be supported by evidence which at least is worthy of consideration? Do They still exist? Here I am going into a line of thought which I should adopt if I were trying to prove to you the existence of any person living in a country which you had not visited, living under conditions which you had not yourself experienced. That it can be absolutely demonstrated in every case I admit to be impossible. I cannot demonstrate to you, for instance, the existence of Count Tolstoi. If you do not travel to Russia, if he does not happen to come here, and you do not happen to meet him, I cannot show you as an absolute matter of demonstration that he exists. But I could bring you evidence that would convince any reasonable man; I could show you evidence which would be admitted in any Court of Law; I could show you that there is no reason for denying his existence merely because you have not personally met him, and therefore obtained what you would call ocular proof of his existence.

H. P. BLAVATSKY

Now what is the proof for the existence of Divine, of Perfect Men living at the present time, reachable under certain conditions? What evidence can I submit to you for that? There are many of you probably who will object to my first witness; but not for the objection am I going to hold back her name—I speak of H. P. Blavatsky. I know the attacks that from every side have been made upon her. I have read the latest attacks that, while I was away, were brought against her, and in face of those, having read, and read them carefully, I say that there remains enough evidence coming through her, untouched by those attacks, sufficient to put before you for your consideration, and sufficient to win the assent of rational men. H. P. Blavatsky is accused of fraud, accused of evil conduct, accused of being nothing more than rogue and charlatan and impostor; but there are certain facts remaining, which you will have to deal with even if you believe, as I do not believe, in the truth of these exaggerated charges that are brought against her. Take if you will, for a moment—though I should deny it—take if you will some of the worst of those charges—that she had no contact with the Mahātmās at all, that she invented Them, that They did not exist outside her imagination, and that everything she said was falsehood, everything that she said and did was intended to mislead. Still you have to deal with the facts of her life, and with the facts of her books.

"THE SECRET DOCTRINE"

You have to deal with the book known as *The Secret Doctrine*, and if you want to understand that you must read it before you waive it aside, and study it before you laugh at it. And I say this on purpose, because I have read the Appendix in which Mr. Coleman says it is full of plagiarisms, that he can prove here, there, and everywhere that she has borrowed from other books her knowledge; he says that would account for the knowledge therein displayed. But what you have to consider is this: that she never claimed that she discovered the knowledge she gave to the world; that her contention is that this knowledge comes down from a far-off past, is found in every Scripture, in every philosophy; and the very purpose of that book is to quote from every direction, from the Scriptures of every religion, from the writings of every people, in order to show the identity of the teaching and to prove the antiquity of the doctrine. What is new in the book is not facts that therein you find. What is new in the book is not what has been found by Orientalists, and may be pointed to in one or another sacred book of the world. What is new is the knowledge which enabled her to select from the whole of these the facts which build up a single, mighty conception of the evolution of the universe, the evolution of man, the coherent synthesis of the whole cosmogony. And that is her title to be the greatest Teacher of our time, because she had real knowledge, not mere book-learning, knowledge which enabled her to collect from scattered books the truths which, fitted together, made one mighty whole; because she held the clue which she was able to follow with unerring accuracy through the maze, and show that all the scattered materials contained within them the possibility of the single building. And her work is the more wonderful because she did it not being a scholar; because she did it not having had the education which would have enabled her to some extent to piece this knowledge together; because she did what no Orientalists have done with all their learning; what not all the Orientalists together have done with all the help of their knowledge of Eastern tongues and their study of Eastern literature. There is not one of them who out of that tangled mass brought out that mighty synthesis; not one of them who out of that chaos was able to build up a cosmos. But this Russian woman with little education, this Russian woman who was no scholar, and pretended to be none, somewhere or other she gained a knowledge that enabled her to do what none of your scholars can do, somewhere or other she had a teaching which enabled her to reduce this chaos to order, and to bring out a mighty scheme of evolution which makes us understand the universe and man. She said it was not hers, she never claimed to have originated it; she was always speaking of her own want of knowledge and referring to Those who taught her.

But the fact you have to meet is this—the knowledge is there, and stands there for criticism. Not one other person has done it, although the same materials that Mr. Coleman says she used are open to the whole of the world. And my answer is: Give us then some others who can do as she did. Let us have some more of this plagiarism which is able to gather from so many sources everything that is necessary for a mighty philosophy. Let your boasted scholars do it, and help us to understand, as she helps us to understand, the religions of the world. Let them show us the identity, let them show us the reality, and then we may begin perhaps to revise our opinion of her; but until that is done her claim remains unshaken, even though you should prove that she may have erred in much, and even although stones may be thrown at her by those who can never rival her in unselfishness, in self-sacrifice and in knowledge.

And the reason that you cannot shake us in our belief in this is because she helped us to knowledge, because we gained from her teaching that which none other gave, because she opened up to us ways of gaining further knowledge along the same lines, and from the same Teachers who had taught her. That is why we remain such fools as people think us, in clinging to her and clinging to her memory, for we owe her a debt of gratitude that we never shall be able to pay, and never shall stone be cast upon her grave which I will not try to lift off it, for the sake of the knowledge to which she led me, and the priceless benefits that she gave me in the teaching which she began.

Now the evidence that I ask you to take from her is not the evidence of phenomena. I put that on one side. It is not the evidence of scholarship. She had none, she never pretended to it. It is not the question as to whether or not her life from her childhood was perfect. It is that she had certain definite knowledge acquired somehow, which cannot be accounted for by ordinary education, which she obtained in a comparatively short space of time, which astonished her own family and friends when first she produced it, and which she said she got from certain Teachers—the important fact being that she possessed it, however it may have come into her possession. That is the evidence that I want to lay stress upon, because that is the point which cannot be shaken, and it removes her testimony for the moment from the whole question of fraud of any sort; it remains above it and beyond it. And I say that even if you think the evidence against her convincing that she went at times beyond the truth—I am not saying it is so, but I am saying, suppose you think the evidence convincing —what then? There remains the fact of this knowledge embodied in *The Secret Doctrine*, which stands there as a witness to her, and which I venture to say cannot be overthrown; and the more you degrade her, the less you make of her, the more you prove the existence of and exalt the Great Ones who worked through her, and gave her what she produced.

"THE VOICE OF THE SILENCE"

Now, there is another point about another book of hers which is to me of special interest, a book that you may know, *The Voice of the Silence*: that book happened to be written while I was with her at Fontainebleau. It is a small book, and in what I am going to say I speak only of the book itself: I am not speaking of the notes; those were done afterwards. The book itself is what may be called a prose poem in three divisions. She wrote it at Fontainebleau, and the greater part was done when I was with her, and I sat in the room while she was writing it. I know that she did not write it referring to any books, but she wrote it down steadily, hour after hour, exactly as though she were writing either from memory or from reading it where no book was. She produced, in the evening, that manuscript that I saw her write as I sat with her, and asked myself and others to correct it for English, for she said that she had written it so quickly that it was sure to be bad. We did not alter in that more than a few words, and it remains as a specimen of marvellously beautiful literary work, putting everything else aside.

Now Mr. Coleman says that he can find this in a number of other books. I can only hope he did not read the book before making that statement. For the book is, as I said, a prose poem, full of spiritual inspiration, full of food for the heart, stimulating the loftiest virtue and containing the noblest ideals. It is not a hotch-potch drawn from various sources, but a coherent, ethical whole. It moves us, not by a statement of facts gathered from books, but by an appeal to the divinest instincts of our nature: it is its own best testimony to the source whence it came.

PERSONAL KNOWLEDGE

Pass now from Madame Blavatsky herself to those she taught. Our Chairman is one of them. Many others are living, here and elsewhere, whom she taught at first, and who have passed from her training into and under the training of her Teachers. And here you have an accumulating testimony of men and women who, of their own authority, by first-hand evidence, out of their own experience, testify to the reality of the existence of these Teachers, and to their own personal knowledge of Them, and of the teaching which they have personally received from Them.

I have mentioned during the last week in two of your papers a small part of my own evidence. Mr. Sinnett to-day in his opening speech has alluded to evidence extending in his own case over fifteen years. Many others have done the same, like Countess Wachtmeister, like Colonel Olcott, like others who have given their own individual testimony. Are you going to say that all these people are frauds? With what right do you so condemn them? Are you going to say that they are all fools? But they are men and women living the ordinary life, men and women who amongst those who know them stand as persons of education, of intelligence, showing the ordinary powers of discrimination and of knowledge that others possess. Are you going to say that we are all mad? That is rather a rash assertion to make against constantly growing numbers of apparently reasonable men and women. What other sort of evidence can you demand for the existence of anyone save the evidence of those who know him, of persons of integrity and of honour who are living amongst yourselves? We bear to These our personal testimony, not founded on documents, not founded on writings, not founded simply on letters, and so on, on which there is always possibility of deception arising, but on individual communion with individual Teachers, and teaching received which otherwise we could not have gained. That is the kind of evidence you have to deal with; and no case of proving fraud against one or two or three people will upset the accumulating testimony of reasonable men and women, who are coming into connection with those Teachers, and who bear testimony to what they themselves know. That is the kind of evidence that you have to meet, that the kind of testimony that you have to overthrow. And however much you may be amused at smart and clever writing, which takes advantage of the deception practised by one in order to discredit the whole, you can no more discredit this mass of testimony by proving one man to be fraudulent, than you can challenge, say, the reality of real coin because a forger may circulate some false coin in a community, and people may pass the coin for the moment, and may be deceived into believing that it is real.

But you may say: We want first-hand evidence for ourselves. You can have it; but you must take the way. You can have the evidence amounting to demonstration for yourselves if you choose to take the trouble, if you choose to give the time. Not an unreasonable demand.

If you want to verify for yourselves the experiments of some great chemist, can you do it by simply going into a laboratory and mixing together the things that you find there? If you want to verify some of the latest experiments in chemical science, do you suppose that you can do it for yourselves, without giving years of trouble and of study to master the science in which you want to carry out a critical experiment? And what would you think of the value of the criticism of some person absolutely ignorant of chemistry, if he said the experiment could not be performed, merely because he was not able to do it without training and without knowledge?

THE WAY TO ADEPTSHIP

Therefore I said that I would tell you how the Mahāṭmā becomes. For only those who are willing to aim at that goal can obtain the absolute demonstration of the existence of Those who have achieved. That is the price that has to be paid. And without this only probability? Yes, reasonable probability; testimony of others which you would accept on any other matter, on which, in a law-court, you would pass vast sums of money, large estates, or anything else; that you can have by simply looking into the available evidence of which I have been sketching merely the outline. But personal demonstration? For that you must begin yourselves to develop in the way in which Their development has been made; and in order that anyone who desires may begin to follow that line and follow it to its natural ending, there have been published to the world the preliminary steps upon the Path, the steps that are taken by those who attain the knowledge, the steps that anyone may begin to take and by which he in his turn may acquire a certainty similar to that which some of us possess. Two little books, especially, have been published, which trace the beginnings of the Path, one called *Light on the Path*, the other, the one to which I before alluded, *The Voice of the Silence*; and in addition to those there are many hints scattered through Theosophical literature, and becoming more and more numerous as the individual experience of disciples increases as the years go on.

How then should ordinary men or women begin? If they desire to get evidence for themselves as to the possibility of this development, which in the end will make the Perfect Man—the man become Divine—the first, the early steps, are those which every religion has taught—carefulness and unselfishness in life, discharge of duty in whatever place in life man or woman may happen to be. To use the phrase which is used in this book[1]: "Follow the wheel of life; follow the wheel of duty to race and kin"; that is a preliminary. For those who would gain knowledge of the Soul must begin in this way, which has ever been taught, by the leaving off of evil ways, and by the following of good; by purity in life, by service to men, by the unselfish effort, continually repeated, to be useful in whatever place one may be in by the law of nature. The endeavour to discharge to the fullest every obligation, the endeavour to live a life which shall leave the world better than it was found, the endeavour to live nobly, unselfishly, and purely—

[1] *The Voice of the Silence.*

these are conditions laid down for those who would find the Path.

REINCARNATION

And here let me say that unless reincarnation be true, then most certainly this development is not possible. In no one human life could that long Path be trodden; in no new-born Soul could be developed these divine possibilities; unless it be true that the Soul of man comes back life after life to earth, bringing with it to every new life the experience of the lives behind, building up higher and higher character life after life, then indeed the Mahāṭmā would be an impossibility, and the perfection of man would be but the dream of the poet. Reincarnation is taken for granted in the whole of this teaching, as a fundamental fact in nature, on which the perfection of the individual must depend.

TO LIVE NOBLY

First then, a man through many lives must set himself to live well, to live usefully, to live nobly, so that he may be born time after time with higher and higher qualities, with nobler and nobler faculties. Next, there is a stage in this human evolution, marked and definite, where the Soul, having long been struggling upwards, raises itself a little beyond the ordinary evolution of man. There are men and women who are exceptionally unselfish, who show exceptional capacities, exceptional intuitions, exceptional love for spiritual things, exceptional devotion to the service of mankind; when those exceptional qualities begin to manifest themselves, then comes the time when one of the great Teachers takes that person in hand individually, in order to guide the further evolution and to train the evolving Soul. The earlier efforts must be made in concert with the great spiritual forces which spread through all the world. But when those have been utilised, when men and women have done their best, as it were, along this line of general spiritual growth, then comes the stage when the Teacher comes forward to guide the further evolution, and certain definite demands are made, if this further evolution is to proceed.

These are laid down in the books to which I alluded. Summed up in a phrase, or rather in two phrases, they might be called "the realisation of non-separateness," which I will explain in a moment, and "rigid self-discipline". Non-separateness on the one side, self-discipline upon the other. Now "non-separateness" is a technical word, which means this: that you realise that you are one fundamentally with all that lives and breathes, that you do not separate yourself from any living thing, that you separate yourself neither from the sinner nor from the saint, neither from the highest nor from the lowest of mankind. Nay, not even from the lower forms of living things, and things called non-living, which you recognise as being one in essence, and one with your innermost Self. How shall it be shown? It is shown by the deliberate attempt and training to begin to identify yourself with the sufferings, with the feelings, and with the wants of man. You are told: "Let thy soul lend its ear to every cry of pain like as the lotus bares its heart to drink the morning sun. Let not the fierce sun dry one tear of pain, before thyself hast wiped it from the sufferer's eye." But that is not all. "Let each burning human tear drop on thy heart and there remain; nor ever brush it off, until the pain that caused it is removed."[1] There is the first note. Go out to the sufferer and relieve his pain; but relieving his pain, let it wring your own heart, and let it remain there as a constant suffering until the cause of that pain has been removed. That is the first stage of non-separateness. Identify yourself with the sorrows and the joys of the world; let the sorrow of every one be your sorrow, the pain of every one your pain, the joy of every one your joy. Your heart, you are told, must answer to every thrill in other hearts, as the string gives back the note of music to which it has been attuned. You must feel the pain, you must feel the agony; nay, you must feel the sin and the shame as your

[1] *The Voice of the Silence.* The other quotations are from the same book.

sin and your shame, and make it part of your own consciousness, and bear it, and never try to escape therefrom. You must train yourself in a sensitiveness which will answer to every suffering of mankind, and you must carry that out in deed as well as in feeling; for you are told again that "Inaction in a deed of mercy becomes an action in a deadly sin." But you must not only realise the pain of the world and make it yours; you must be as hard to yourself as you are tender to those around. You have no time to spend on your own troubles, if the trouble of the world is to become yours. You have no strength to waste on laments over your own grief, if you are to be identified with the sorrows of mankind. And so it is said that you must be as hard as the stone of the mango-fruit to your own pains and sorrows, while soft as its pulp to the pains and sorrows of other men.

BROTHERHOOD

And thus life after life you must be trained, life after life becoming more and more identified with all, and breaking down everything that separates man from man. That is why brotherhood is our only condition; because the recognition of that is the first step towards this realisation of non-separateness, which is necessary if the disciple is to progress. And the definite training of the disciple is a training which makes him sensitive to the sorrows of all, in order that, feeling, he may be ready to help, and which trains him in this self-identification with the whole, in order that he may at last become one of the Saviours of the world. For as this training proceeds life after life, there gradually develops in this human being an ever-growing sympathy, an ever-deepening compassion, a charity which nothing can stain, and a tolerance which nothing can shake. No injury can give offence, for the sorrow is for the one who does the injury, and not for the blow which is struck at oneself. No anger can arise against any wrong, for you understand why the wrong is done, and you sorrow for the doer and have no time to waste in anger. You will not condone wrong, you will not say that wrong is right, you will not pretend that good is evil, for that would be the greatest cruelty and would make the progress of the race impossible. But while recognising the evil, there will be no anger against the evil-doer, for he is one with your own Soul, and you recognise no separation between yourself and him.

To what end? Because, as this growth proceeds, memory and knowledge will grow; because, as this growth proceeds, the developing life of the Spirit within the disciple will show itself out more and more in the walks of men, and gradually he will become marked out as a worker for man, a helper for man, a toiler for man, working for him to enlighten his ignorance, to bring him knowledge, and to show him the reality that underlies all the illusions in the world. And he must be hard to himself because he is to stand between man and evil, because he is to stand between his weaker brothers and the dark powers that otherwise might crush them. The illustrations given here of what the disciple must be are that he is to be like a Star which gives light to all, but takes from none; that he is to be like the snow which takes on itself the frost and the biting winds, in order that the seeds below may sleep uninjured by the cold, and have the possibility of growth when the season for growth shall come. There is the training to which submission is demanded by these Divine Teachers; there what they claim from men who desire to be disciples. Not accomplishment at first, but endeavour; not perfection at first, but effort; not certainly the showing out of the ideal, but the striving after it amid whatever failure and amid whatever error. And I ask you if those of us who realise this as ideal, and who know that this is the demand which our Teachers make upon us, is it likely that we should act for the injury of society, or be anything save the servants of men in obedience to Those whose law we strive to obey?

And then, as I said, life after life these qualities develop, until there comes at last a time when the weaknesses of men have fallen away, when the frailties of human nature have gradually been overcome, when a compassion that nothing can shake, a purity that nothing can soil, a knowledge mighty in its scope, and a spirituality that makes itself felt—when these are the qualities that mark the disciple who is nearing the threshold of liberation; until the day dawns when the treading of this Path is finished, the time comes when the disciple's course is over, and the last possibility of the Perfect Man opens before his eyes. And then for a while the earth, as it were, drops into the background; he stands—the liberated Soul as he is called, the Soul that has won his freedom, the Soul that has conquered human limitations—he stands on the threshold of Nirvāṇa, of that perfect consciousness and bliss which go beyond possibility of human thought, which go beyond possibility of our limited consciousness. And as he stands there it has been said that there is silence; silence in Nature, one of whose children is rising beyond her, silence which nothing for a time may break, when the liberated Soul has accomplished his freedom. Silence—and it is broken by a voice: it is a voice that unites into one mighty cry the whole of the misery of the world which has been left behind. A cry from the world in its darkness, in its misery, in its spiritual starvation, in its moral degradation. And in that silence surrounding the liberated Soul, the cry that comes across is the cry of misery from the human race to the Soul that has gone beyond his brothers, to the Soul that is free while they are left in chains.

THE SENSE OF UNITY

How shall he go further? Life after life he has learned to identify himself with man; life after life he has learned to answer to every cry of pain. Can he go onward freed, and leave others in chains? Can he go onward into bliss, and leave the world in sorrow? He whom we call the Mahāṭmā is the liberated Soul who has the right to go onward, but for Love's sake turns back, who brings His knowledge to the helping of ignorance, brings His purity to the cleansing of foulness, brings His light to the chasing away of darkness, and takes up again the burden of the flesh till all the race of men shall be free with Him, and He shall go onward not alone, but as father of a mighty family, bringing humanity with Him to share the common goal and the common bliss in Nirvāṇa. That is the Mahāṭmā. Life after life of effort crowned with supreme renunciation; perfection gained by struggle and by toil, and then brought back to help others till they stand where He is standing. Every Soul that stretches out its hands, His hand is ready to help. Of every brother of His race that asks for guidance, His heart answers to the cry; and They stand there waiting until we are willing to be taught, and give Them the opportunity which They have renounced Nirvāṇa to secure.

A SUBLIME IDEAL

Is that an ideal for scoffing, for laughter, for idle ridicule? If it be only a dream, it is the noblest dream that humanity has ever dreamed; the fullest of self-sacrifice, and the most inspiring of ideals. To some a fact—a fact more real than life. But to those to whom it is no fact it might be an ideal; an ideal of self-sacrifice, of knowledge, and of love. That such Men are, some of us know. But even if you believe not in Them, there is nothing in the ideal that is not noble, and by thinking of which you may not grow higher and higher towards the light.

The Christian has the same ideal in his Christ; the Buḍḍhist the same ideal in his Buḍḍha. Every faith has the same ideal in the Man whom it regards as Divine. And we stand as witness to all religions that their faith is real and not false; their Teachers a reality, and not a dream; for the Teacher is the realisation of the promise in the disciple, the realisation of the ideal that we adore. And so to some of us these Divine Teachers, whom we know to live, are a daily inspiration. We can only come in contact with Them as we strive to purify ourselves. We can only learn more as we practise what already They have taught. And if I have spoken here to-night at first of a theory, then of the historical past, then of the witness that we bear you in the present, and lastly of the steps that all may take if they will, it is because I want to lift the ideal out of all the ridicule that has been heaped upon it, away from all the mud that has been cast upon it, out of the jar and the strife which has been made to surround it.

Blame us as you will, but leave that noble ideal of human perfection untouched. Laugh at us as you will, but do not laugh at the Perfect Man, the man made God, in whom, after all, the most of you believe. Do not, you who are Christians, be false to your own religion, and leave your Christ only as a matter of faith and not of living reality, as many of you know that He is to-day. And remember that whatever the name, the ideal is the same, whatever the title, the thought that underlies it is identical.

And as you think, you develop; as is your ideal, so gradually your lives will become. For there is this transforming power in thought, that if your ideals are paltry your lives will be paltry; if your ideals are material your lives will be material. Take then this ideal and think of it, and your lives will become penetrated by its purity; you will become the nobler men and the nobler women, because it forms a subject of your thought, and the thought transforms you into its own likeness. It is true that men become like that they worship; it is true that men become like that on which they think. And this ideal of the Perfect Man has in it the hope for the future of the race. Therefore I plead for it to you to-day, and I point you to the Path by which from an ideal it may become a living reality, turning from a hope into a living Teacher, and from a lofty ideal for aspiration into the Friend and the Master to whom you may give your life.

THE ADEPTS

WHO IS THE MASTER?

AMONG the many questions to which Theosophy gives rise, none perhaps awakens more interest and arouses more enquiry than that of the Masters. What is indicated by the term? Who are They? Where do They live? What do They do? These, and many other questions, are constantly heard. Let me try to throw a little light on these questions, to answer them, at least, partially.

A Master is a term applied by Theosophists to denote certain human beings, who have completed their human evolution, have attained human perfection, have nothing more to learn so far as our part of the solar system is concerned, have reached what the Christians call "Salvation," and the Hindūs and Buddhists "Liberation". When the Christian Church still kept "the faith once delivered to the Saints" in its fulness, salvation meant much more than escape from everlasting damnation. It meant the release from compulsory reincarnation, safety from all possibility of failure in evolution. "To him that overcometh" was the promise that he should be "a pillar in the Temple of my God, and *he shall go out no more*". He that had overcome was "saved".

The conception of evolution, which implies a gradual expansion of consciousness, embodied in ever-improving material forms, underlies the conception of Masterhood. The perfection it connotes is to be reached by every human being, and clearly perfection cannot be gained in the course of one brief human life. The differences between man and man, between genius and dolt, between saint and criminal, between athlete and cripple, are only reconcilable with the divine justice if each human being is in course of growth from savagery to nobility, and if these differences are merely the signs of differing stages of that growth. At the apex of such a long evolution stands the "Master," embodying in himself the highest results possible to man of intellectual, moral, and spiritual development. He has learned all the lessons that humanity can assimilate, and the value of all the experience the world can give is His. Beyond this point, evolution is superhuman; if the conqueror returns to human life it is a voluntary action, for neither birth can seize him nor death touch him, save by his own consent.

We must add something to this for the full conception of Masterhood. The Master must be in a human body, must be incarnate. Many who reach this level no longer take up the burden of the flesh, but using only "the spiritual body" pass out of touch with this earth, and inhabit only loftier realms of existence. Further, a Master —as the name implies—takes pupils, and in strictness the term should only be applied to those who discharge the special function of helping less advanced men and women to tread the arduous road which takes them "by a short cut" to the summit of human evolution, far in advance of the bulk of their fellow-men. Evolution has been compared to a road winding round and round a hill in an ascending spiral, and along that road humanity slowly advances; there is a short cut to the top of the hill, straight, narrow, rugged and steep, and "few there be that find it". Those few are the pupils, or "disciples" of the Masters. As in the days of the Christ, they must "forsake all and follow Him".

Those who are at this level, but do not take pupils, are concerned in other lines of service to the world, whereof something will presently be said. There is no English name to distinguish these from the teachers, and so, perforce, the word Master is applied to them also. In India, where these various functions are known as coming down from a remote antiquity, there are different names for the different functions, but it would be difficult to popularise these in English.

We may take, then, as a definition of a Master: a human being who has perfected himself and has nothing more to learn on earth, who lives in a physical body on earth for the helping of man, who takes pupils that desire to evolve more rapidly than their race, in order to serve it, and are willing to forsake all for this purpose.

THE PERFECT MAN: HIS PLACE IN EVOLUTION

It may, perhaps, be necessary to add, for the information of those who are not familiar with the Theosophical conception of evolution, that when we say "a perfect man" we mean a good deal more than is generally connoted by the phrase. We mean a consciousness which is able to function unbrokenly through the five great spheres in which evolution is proceeding: the physical, intermediate and heavenly worlds, to which all men are now related, and in addition to these the two higher heavens—St. Paul, it may be remembered, speaks of the "third heaven"—which ordinary humanity cannot as yet enter. A Master's consciousness is at home in all these and includes them all, and his refined and subtle bodies function freely in them all, so that he can at any time know and act at will in any part of any one of them.

The grade occupied by the Masters is the fifth in the great Brotherhood, the members of which have outpaced normal evolution. The four lower grades consist of initiated disciples, who live and labour for the most part unknown in the everyday world, carrying on the work assigned to them by their superiors. At certain times in human history, in serious crises, in the transitions from one type of civilisation to another, members of the Occult Hierarchy, Masters and even loftier Beings, come out into the world; normally, although incarnate, they remain in retired and secluded spots, away from the tumult of human life, in order to carry on the helpful work which would be impossible of accomplishment in the crowded haunts of men.

THE MASTER JESUS

Jesus—during the first thirty years of His life, before His baptism, when the "Spirit of God" descended upon Him and thenceforth abode in Him, raising the human body to be the Temple of the incarnate Christ—was the purest and holiest of disciples, and thereafter, as man, achieved Masterhood, and became the Lord and Master of the Church founded by the Christ. It is significant that in the Church belief, the reality of the continuing human body is laid stress upon, "*wherewith* He ascended into heaven". Through all the troubled ages of Christianity, the Master Jesus has been the Guardian and Shepherd of His Church, guiding, inspiring, disciplining, purifying, century after century, and now pouring forth the stream of mystic Christianity which is watering the garden of Christendom and causing fair blossoms to flower forth once more. Clothed in a body He has taken from Syria, He is waiting the time for His reappearance in the open life of men.

THE MASTER HILARION

Hilarion—once Iamblichus of the Neo-Platonic Schools, who gave through M. C. *Light on the Path*, and through H. P. Blavatsky *The Voice of the Silence*, skilled craftsman in poetic English prose and in melodious utterance--is labouring also for the coming time, and will play his part in the drama of the New Age.

THE MASTERS M. AND K. H.

Those who are named M. and K.H. in *The Occult World* by Mr. Sinnett were the two Masters who founded the Theosophical Society, using Colonel H. S. Olcott and H. P. Blavatsky, both disciples of M., to lay its foundation; and who gave to Mr. Sinnett the materials from which he wrote his famous books—the one named above, and *Esoteric Buddhism*—which brought the light of Theosophy to thousands in the West. H. P. Blavatsky has told how she met the Master M. on the bank of the Serpentine, when she visited London in 1851.

THE MASTER RAKOCZI AND OTHERS

The last survivor of the Royal House of Rakoczi, known as the Comte de S. Germain in the history of the eighteenth century; as Bacon in the seventeenth; as Robertus, the monk, in the sixteenth; as Hunyadi Janos in the fifteenth; as Christian Rosencreuz in the fourteenth—to take a few of his incarnations—was disciple through these laborious lives and now has achieved Masterhood, the "Hungarian Adept" of *The Occult World*, and known to some of us in that Hungarian body.

And there is "the Venetian," and "Serapis" who taught Colonel Olcott for a while, and "the Old Gentleman of Tiruvallur," that H. P. Blavatsky named thus quaintly, visited in his Nilgiri retreat by Subba Row and C. W. Leadbeater, the retreat some eighty miles from Adyar, where he lives secluded, watching the world as it changes, and plunging deeply into the abstruser sciences of which chemistry and astronomy are the outer shells.

These are some of the Masters, more or less publicly known, and to be known more publicly ere the present century is numbered with the past.

WHERE DO THEY LIVE?[1]

They live in different countries, scattered over the world. The Master Jesus lives mostly in the

[1] [A fuller account is given in *The Masters and the Path* by C. W. Leadbeater.]

mountains of Lebanon; the Master Hilarion in Egypt—he wears a Cretan body; the Masters M. and K. H. in Tibet, near Shigatse, both using Indian bodies; the Master Rakoczi in Hungary, but travelling much; I do not know the dwelling-places of "the Venetian" and the Master "Serapis". Dwelling-places of the physical body seem to mean so little when the swift movements of the subtle body, freed at will from the grosser one, carry the owner whither he wills at any time. "Place" loses its ordinary significance to those who are free denizens of space, coming and going at will. And though one knows that they have abiding-places where dwells usually the physical body, that body is so much of a vesture, at any moment to be readily laid aside, that the "where" loses its interest to a great extent.

THEIR WORK

They aid, in countless ways, the progress of humanity. From the highest sphere they shed down light and life on all the world, that may be taken up and assimilated, as freely as the sunshine, by all who are receptive enough to take it in. As the physical world lives by the life of God, focused by the sun, so does the spiritual world live by that same life, focused by the Occult Hierarchy. Next, the Masters specially connected with religions use these reilgions as reservoirs into which they pour spiritual energy, to be distributed to the faithful in each religion through the duly appointed "means of grace". Next comes the great intellectual work, wherein the Masters send out thought-forms of high intellectual power to be caught up by men of genius, assimilated by them and given out to the world; on this level also they send out their wishes to their disciples, notifying them of the tasks to which they should set their hands. Then comes the work in the lower mental world, the generation of the thought-forms which influence the concrete mind and guide it along useful lines of activity in this world, and the teaching of those who are living in the heavenly world. Then the large activities of the intermediate world, the helping of the so-called dead, the general direction and supervision of the teaching of the younger pupils and the sending of aid in numberless cases of need. In the physical world the watching of the tendencies of events, the correction and neutralising, as far as law permits, of evil currents, the constant balancing of the forces that work for and against evolution, the strengthening of the good, the weakening of the evil. In conjunction with the Angels of the Nations also they work, guiding the spiritual forces as the others guide the material, choosing and rejecting actors in the great Drama, influencing the councils of men, supplying needful impulses in the right direction.

These are but a few of the activities ceaselessly carried on in every sphere by the Guardians of humanity, some of the activities which come within our limited vision. They stand as a Guardian Wall around humanity, within which it can progress, uncrushed by the tremendous cosmic forces which play around our planetary house. From time to to time, one of them comes forth into the world of men, as a great religious teacher, to carry on the task of spreading a new form of the Eternal Verities, a form suitable to a new race or civilisation. Their ranks include all the greatest Prophets of the Faiths of the world, and while a religion lives one of these great Ones is ever at its head, watching over it as His special charge.

THE WORLD-TEACHER

During the present century, one of those great crises in the history of humanity will occur, which mark the conception of a new civilisation. He whom in the East men call the Wisdom-Truth, the World-Teacher, and whom in the West men call the Christ, will ere long return incarnate upon earth and move once more among the busy crowds of men. With Him will come several of the Masters, to aid His work and spread abroad His message. The hurrying rush of present events, the intolerable burdens crushing down the peoples, menace of war, the chaos of opinions, political, social, and religious; all these and many more are the signs of the changing times, of the passing away of the old, of the birthing of the new. It will, indeed, be a new world on which the eyes of the infants of to-day will gaze in their maturity; for again is ringing forth the ancient saying: "Behold! I create a new heaven and a new earth. Behold! I make all things new."

Printed and published by A. K. Sitarama Shastri,